BEING
YOU

For Mollie and Ziggy
Always be you,
whoever that may be!

– DANIEL THOMPSON

BEING YOU

POEMS of POSITIVITY

written by
Daniel Thompson

illustrated by
Julia Murray

Contents

Every morning when you wake,
There're two yous you can be.
The second costs an awful lot,
The first's already free.

The second takes all day to do,
The first's already done.
The second has a lot at stake,
The first is rather fun.

The second leads to worry,
Scrutinising what you've said.
The first is freely thinking,
Wondrous thoughts inside your head.

So every morning when you wake,
Which person will you be?
Will you act like someone else?
Or just say I AM ME!

LIVE LIFE iN COLOUR

Think of your life,
As a sketch drawn in pencil.
An outline of where to begin.
A near blank canvas,
Of endless potential,
And your job's to colour it in!

But not with a crayon,
And not with a pen.
No, the marvellous colours you'll use,
Are found in the moments,
Between now and then,
Of the life that you lovingly choose.

There's colour in smiling,
And laughing too much,
In success when you're out of your depth.
There's colour in love,
And its delicate touch,
And the moments you didn't expect.

There's colour in travelling,
And seeing the world,
In the words of the minds you admire.

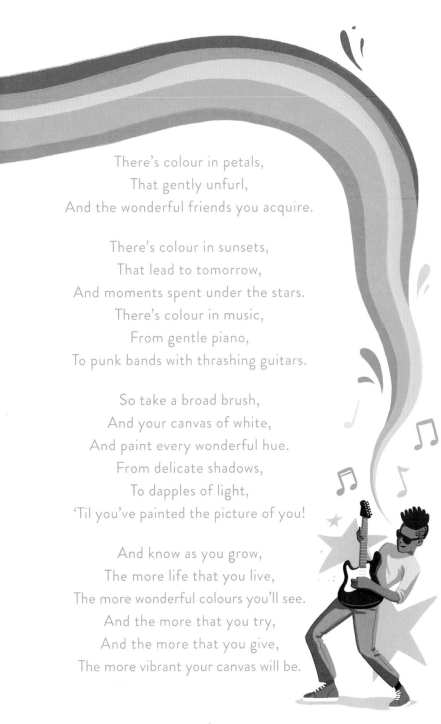

There's colour in petals,
That gently unfurl,
And the wonderful friends you acquire.

There's colour in sunsets,
That lead to tomorrow,
And moments spent under the stars.
There's colour in music,
From gentle piano,
To punk bands with thrashing guitars.

So take a broad brush,
And your canvas of white,
And paint every wonderful hue.
From delicate shadows,
To dapples of light,
'Til you've painted the picture of you!

And know as you grow,
The more life that you live,
The more wonderful colours you'll see.
And the more that you try,
And the more that you give,
The more vibrant your canvas will be.

FOLLOW YOUR

DREAMS

If you think you've found your focus,
And you're hanging on a dream.
Don't wait until you're noticed,
Go ahead and make some steam.

You don't have to ask permission,
So displace your grace and poise.
Make fate your own decision,
Go ahead and make some noise.

Let people know you're coming,
Quietly waiting rarely pays.
Get loudly up and running,
Go ahead and make some waves.

Stop hiding in the covers,
Be the roll of your own wheel.
Don't leave your dreams to others,
Go ahead and make them real.

KEEP GROWING

Some people try to put you down,
By telling you you've changed.
But nothing born upon this Earth,
Is meant to stay the same.

Just think about the butterfly,
Who flutters by and know.
Sometimes, no matter who you are,
You have to change to grow.

MAKE THiNGS HAPPEN

When circumstance provides a glance,
Of something that you crave.
Go take your shot with all you've got,
Be confident and brave.

Don't waste your time, don't wait on signs,
Don't look for hidden patterns.
The perfect time is always now,
So go and make things happen.

Don't play it safe to save some face,
Just give yourself a shove.
You can fail at what you hate,
So do the thing you love.

BE CURIOUS

Now I need to be honest here, right off the bat,
Curiosity possibly has killed a cat.
Or two, or three. But here's a fact,
Curiosity's given us much more than that.

It's the reason you're you, it's the reason we're here,
And perhaps you can't see it but let me be clear.
From the edges of space to the depths of the ocean,
Curiosity comes in perpetual motion.

It's every invention you might care to mention,
From motor car rumbles to rocket ascension.

It powers computers, it choreographs dances,
It's medical marvels and wondrous advances.

It's the weight of an apple, the scientist's beaker,
The roof of the chapel, the call of eureka!
It forms the foundations of deep conversations,
And senses vibrations in far constellations.

It walks to the poles, it discovers new nations,
Climbs mountains, builds fountains, exceeds expectations.
It's fabric, it's dinner, it's riding your bike,
It's aeroplanes, music, electrical lights.

It's taking a chance, and it's daring to dream,
It's being yourself, whatever that means.
And perhaps curiosity sealed the cat's fate,
But it's also the reason that people are great.

So I'm willing to risk making feline fans furious,
As I strongly advise you to always be curious.

Panic and worry show up in a hurry,
Long before reason or rhyme.
Your feet start to pace and your mind starts to race,
As an army of thoughts seize your mind.

And it's hard to stay calm, and it's hard to stay strong,
And it's easy to focus on how it's gone wrong.
As a spiral of doubt pulls you further below,
Convinced of a worst-case scenario.

And yes, there's a chance that you might be correct,
And things will unfold in the way you expect.
But time after time you will find your position,
Will end up less scary than what you envision.

And mostly you'll manage, and mostly you'll cope,
And mostly things work out the way you would hope.
And mostly you'll notice when all's done and said,
The worry and panic was just in your head.

So rather than twisting yourself in a knot,
Stop for a second, breathe deep and take stock.
Wait for the outcome, and mostly you'll find,
Life will continue and things will be fine.

If you're wanting to win a gold medal,
Or fly to the moon on a ship.
Or work in a zoo, or be smarter than you,
Take heed of this noteworthy tip.

If ever you think 'I can't do that,'
It's important to never forget.
There isn't a something that you cannot do,
Just a something you cannot do yet.

And it sounds a cliché, but just practise each day,
Let the hours turn the weeks into months.
And a moment will come, when that thing will become,
Just a thing that you couldn't do once.

Changes come slow, but just give it a go,
And I'm certain one day if you do.
You'll find in the mirror, a vaguely familiar,
Better, more interesting you.

LEAVE WORRIES BEHIND

Think of worries,
　　Inside your head,
As useless bags,
　　Of rocks instead.

They may be yours,
　　But have no doubt.
They'll weigh you down,
　　And wear you out.

So let them go!
　　Leave them behind!
It's odd at first,
　　But soon you'll find.

The less you carry,
The less you weigh.
The more you're free,
To enjoy your day.

THE PERSON UNDERNEATH

Some people have dimples,
Or freckles, or pimples,
Big noses, small ears or no teeth.
But it's not who you are,
On the surface that counts,
It's the person who lives underneath.

HOW TO TREAT OTHERS

Treat others as you'd like to be treated,
That's always a good place to start.

But treat them as *they'd* like to be treated,
And you'll find a place in their heart.

JUST

BREATHE

Most people suffer anxieties,
That's something we don't say.
It comes in many varieties,
And if one finds you, that's okay.

It doesn't make you silly,
It doesn't make you strange.
It's perfectly acceptable,
And you don't need to change.

But here's a tip that I was taught,
That you might not believe.
You can find your way to calm,
If you just sit and breathe.

I know it sounds ridiculous,
But really, this one's true.
Once you control your breathing,
You'll regain control of you.

So find a spot and take a seat,
And focus on your breath.
And feel your panic fade away,
Until there's nothing left.

CARRY COMPASSION

Carry compassion,

Over hilltops and valleys,

Mountains and oceans.

Plant it in furrows,

And forests of evergreen,

Sow it in gardens.

Share it with others,

In moments of emptiness,

Offer it freely.

Nurture its beauty.

STAY WEiRD

If you're worried you're weird,
You probably are.
But don't be disheartened at all.

The weird are revered,
The weird are the stars.
The weird are the coolest of cool.

It's not to be feared,
Or carried with strife.
It just means expressing yourself.

So, go and be weird,
You're not meant for a life,
Being normal like everyone else.

From local shops,
To mountain tops,
To lives you won't forget.
Every journey,
That you take,
Begins with just one step.

At first it seems,
Your hopes and dreams,
Are miles and miles away.
But with each step,
You'll find you get,
Much closer every day.

KEEP MOVING FORWARDS

When crossroads come,
You might succumb,
To doubt and hesitation.
But pick your path,
And don't look back,
Head t'wards your destination.

And walk your miles,
With style and smiles,
Through forests, fields and orchards.
Refuse to stop!
You'll find your spot,
If you keep moving forwards.

ASK FOR

Knowing your strengths,
And your strongest events,
Might suggest that you'll be a safe bet.

But knowing your weakness,
Presents a completeness,
That may offer more of a threat.

For those who accept,
What their weakness affects,
Have the ace of the pack up their sleeve.

HELP

Unhampered by pride,
They can seek out a guide,
And can ask for the help that they need.

So identify weak spots,
The don't knows and have nots,
Examine the cards you were dealt.

You'll find you evolve,
With each problem you solve,
Once you learn how to ask for some help.

LiTTLE ACTS
OF KiNDNESS

Those little acts of kindness,
Picking litter off the floor.
Those little acts of kindness,
Taking time to hold the door.
Those little acts of kindness,
Wiping tears from someone's face.
Those little acts of kindness,
They define the human race.

Those little acts of kindness,
Smiling sweetly as you pass.
Those little acts of kindness,
Sharing chocolate, whilst it lasts.
Those little acts of kindness,
Bringing shopping from the car.
Those little acts of kindness,
They remind us who we are.

Those little acts of kindness,
Hugs for friends who feel down.
Those little acts of kindness,
Handing in that phone you found.
Those little acts of kindness,
So petite you'll barely stop.
Those little acts of kindness,
Often mean an awful lot.

Those little acts of kindness,
Saying hi to someone new.
Those little acts of kindness,
Take such little time to do.
Those little acts of kindness,
Made by every boy and girl.
Those little acts of kindness,
Big enough to change the world.

iT'S OKAY

It's okay to change your mind,
It's okay to change your style.
It's okay to change your haircut,
Every once in every while.

It's okay to change your trainers,
It's okay to change your view.
It's okay to change completely,
And it isn't only you.

Because, everything is changing,
Every cloud that passes by,
Gently paints a shifting picture,
As it sails across the sky.

The moon out in the distance,
Changes every single night,

TO CHANGE

And yet we gaze on every phase,
With wonder and delight.

The coast is always changing,
Shifting sands along the shore.
The mountain tall and mighty,
Once lay flat upon the floor.

The city built of concrete,
Stood where nature used to stay.
The universe expanding,
Slightly further every day.

So embrace the way you're changing,
I know it might sound strange.
But in life the only constant,
Is that things must always change.

From Kings and Queens to broken dreams,
One thing I've come to know.
There's no-one born above you,
And there's no-one born below.

We're equal people passing through,
Each trying to do that thing we do.
So stand up tall, reject that label,
You're perfectly able to sit at this table.

Just believe in yourself,
And assume that you can.
Who cares if you can't,
And things don't go to plan.

Just believe in yourself,
There's so much you'll miss out.
If you waste all your moments,
On fear and doubt.

Just believe in yourself,
And assume that you will.
Who cares if you can't,
Taking part is the thrill.

Just believe in yourself,
And grab hold of the baton.
A confident mindset,
Can make something happen.

EVERY LOSS
iS A
WiN

Of course you'd never choose to lose,
But should you take your turn.
Don't think of it as losing,
But instead a chance to learn.

If you can find the reason why,
For every time you lose.
You'll quickly see where things went wrong,
And how you might improve.

Get comfortable with losing,
It's perfectly okay.
Not everyone who's good at something,
Started out that way.

Be humble when you're losing,
And find the words to say.
A better competitor finished ahead,
And today simply wasn't my day.

So next time you lose,
Take your bruise with a smile,
And learn from the lessons within.

And when you look back,
Every once in a while,
You'll see every loss was a win.

PiCK GOOD FRiENDS

Funny friends, happy friends,
Meet you at the weekend friends.
Homework friends, teamwork friends,
Friends you've known a while.

Playground friends, stay 'round friends,
Make you feel fantastic friends.
Honest friends, 'I promise' friends,
Friends who make you smile.

So who's for you? Well that depends,
They come in many types.
And it's your job to meet them all,
And pick the ones you like!

Yes, pick the ones who choose to give,
And ask for nothing back.
Pick the ones who make you feel,
There's strength inside your pack.

Pick the ones who make you laugh,
Until it's hard to breathe.
Pick the ones you see all day,
But still don't want to leave.

Pick the ones who hold your secrets,
Closer than their own.
Pick the ones who sit with you,
On days you feel alone.

And after you have picked your friends,
And learned each face and name.
Make sure that you are their friend too,
And treat them just the same.

TRAIN YOUR

BRAIN

In matters of the self, above everything else,
Take measures to treasure your own mental health.
For your brain, like your body, I have little doubt,
Is made to be strong but it needs to work out.

So take your brain jogging, through riddles and puzzles,
And lift heavy questions to build your brain muscles.
Eat five facts a day for a balanced opinion,
Try not to consume too much junk television.

Take regular laughter and stretch out your smile,
Pick up a new skill every once in a while.
Have fun with your friends and be good to each other,
Take regular rest so your brain can recover.

Add good conversation to every meal,
And find a safe place to express how you feel.
Be kind to yourself and acknowledge each gain,
And drink lots of water, it's good for your brain.

Be generous with compliments,
To everyone you meet.
It barely takes a second,
But you might just make their week.

Be generous with compliments,
It doesn't cost a penny.
Especially if you think perhaps,
They don't receive that many.

Be generous with compliments,
It barely burns a calorie.
Tell your friend her art belongs,
On walls inside a gallery.

Be generous with compliments,
Tell Mum you think she's strong.
Tell Dad his morning cuddles,
Make you feel like you belong.

Be generous with compliments,
Point out your favourite trait.
Be the reason for their smile,
Be why they're feeling great.

Now and then you'll meet someone,
Who's out to test your mettle.
And you might feel an anger rise,
And bubble like a kettle.
A surging urge to go berserk,
And sting them like a nettle.
But wait a beat, before you pour,
Just let your kettle settle.

Take a walk,
Or count to 10.
A deep breath in...
Then out again.

I know it's hard, of course it is,
But all those scalding bubbles,
Rarely get you anywhere,
But into further troubles.
So let your kettle settle,
And once your waters calm,
You'll find you're better placed to face,
The world with grace and charm.

BEING DIFFERENT

There's a curious thing about people,
From our toes to our family name.
In some ways we're nothing like anyone else,
And in others, we're all just the same.

We all have a body,
We all have a brain.
One heart, two lungs,
And blood in our veins.

But at the same time,
You are here on your own,
Your every hair,
And your every bone,

Is yours and yours only,
And it's perfectly true.
You'll never find someone,
Exactly like you.

You're out on your own,
And you're in with the crowd.
You walk your own path,
But you share the same ground.

So don't think of boxes,
Or labels, or names.
No! Nobody's different,
And no-one's the same.

So be open-minded,
Give people a shot.
And then just decide,
If you like them or not.

'Practice makes perfect' requires a correction,
There's more to improvement than reaching perfection.

Some people who practise will never be perfect,
And don't mind at all, and they still think it's worth it.

Some practise for purpose, some practise for pleasure,
Some people get better, some don't even measure.

No, I'd rather tell you that practice make progress,
Forget about perfect and follow the process.

There's more to a mountain than reaching the top,
There're vistas and wonders wherever you stop.

So enjoy what you do, keep your passion intact,
And if you see progress, you're on the right track.

BIOLUMINESCENCE

My favourite word, I've ever heard,
And I do have a preference.
Is not *ice-cream* or *football-team*,
It's *bioluminescence*.
Now some of you may know that word,
But if you don't, in essence...

It means to make a light within,
And have it shine from out your skin.

Glow worms do it, fireflies too,
Beneath the waves there're quite a few.

And though I know your skin won't glow,
It's still a word you ought to know.

Because there is a way in spite,
That you can still emit your light.

Love yourself, and be yourself,
And once you learn that lesson,
A light within, will reach your brim,
Until you're incandescent.
And everywhere you ever go,
You'll glow with iridescence.

And so you see, that's how to be...
Bioluminescent.

THE IMPORTANCE OF PERSPECTIVE

I can't do it!
So I'll pay no attention to the people who tell me
I can achieve anything.
The truth is
I should give up.
And I won't let anyone convince me
Success will be mine.
I know
Whatever I decide to try
Will not happen.
Failure
Will find me.
Happiness
Is impossible.
Nothing
In my future
Will go as I have planned.
Today
I am going to fail.
Only a fool would believe
I can do it.

*Now read it from bottom to top for a change of perspective.

Here's a secret I recently found,
That could help keep your feet on the ground.
Life's about balance,
No matter your talents,
Without it you'll likely fall down.

Think of the humble oak table,
With three legs it stands if it's able.
With two it will sprawl,
And with one it will fall,
But with four legs beneath, it is stable.

Now I'd hazard to make an assertion,
The same rules apply to a person.
For when someone fails,
To balance their scales,
They wibble and wobble and worsen.

So balance your day with a delicate blend,
Of laughter and love with your family and friends.
Work hard to get wealthy,
Work out to stay healthy,
And rest when the day finds an end.

GIVE YOURSELF PURPOSE

The meaning of life is hard to define,
And so far has eluded the greatest of minds.
Some think it's luck, some praise the divine,
There are lots of ideas, and this one is mine.

I think we're stardust, assembled by chance,
Millennia passed and we got quite advanced.
And existence, in essence, appears to be surplus,
And as such we wake up and give ourselves purpose.

But life isn't pointless, no never be fooled,
There're endless distractions to keep
you enthralled.
So give yourself purpose, do what you adore,
Find things that excite you and make
you want more.

And that might not mean an extravagant car,
Or the fame and the fortunes of being a star.
Yes, life might be nice with a mountain of money,
But purpose is something you feel in your tummy.

So give yourself purpose, define who you are,
If you can do that you won't have to go far.
You will spring from your bed with a positive feeling,
For those who have purpose will find they have meaning.

NEVER GiVE UP

Resilience is climbing a mountain,
With obstacles not on your map.
And the voices that echo behind you,
Suggest that you'd better come back.

When you're beaten and battered by weather,
And you'd rather be tucked up in bed.
But still you go on with your journey,
Until there's a summit ahead.

'Til one day you look on the valleys,
So proud that you didn't stay stuck.
Resistance was crucial,
Persistence was fruitful,
And you, well you never gave up.

FORGIVE & FORGET

The problem with hatred,
No matter how just.
Is it clings to your hinges,
And turns them to rust.

You find yourself thinking,
Of what made you mad.
And miss out completely,
On fun to be had.

And the more you stay still,
And obsess on your hate.
The more you'll rust up,
Like a creaky old gate.

So here is the secret,
To oiling your joints.
Don't plan your revenge,
And don't try to score points.

Just let the hate go,
Forgive them regardless.
They may not deserve it,
But show them a kindness.

It won't change the past,
But you'll find in good time.
It will oil your hinges,
And free up your mind.

EVERY WEAKNESS
HiDES A STRENGTH

Now you might have a flaw you hate,
That causes you frustration.
A weakness that you think you have,
In certain situations.

But I'd suggest, that once confessed,
Our flaws are quite subjective.
And all that makes a flaw or strength,
Is merely your perspective.

Let's say today, there was a play,
The shy retiring type,
Might sooner lift the curtain,
Than be thrust beneath the light.

But should the lead in time of need,
Require a listening ear,
That quiet hand might understand,
And help to quell their fear.

So is it weak, to fail to speak,
Beneath a spotlight glistening?
Or is there strength in making sense,
Of those in need by listening?

And so the revelation comes,
And it may leave you speechless.
Every weakness hides a strength,
And every strength, a weakness.

YOU'RE ALREADY
A WINNER

The odds of you walking on Earth,
As it floats through the warmth of the sun.
Are 400 trillion 600 million,
300 thousand to 1.

Now that is like winning the lotto,
Not once, but each time that you play.
It's meeting a shark, as you exit a park,
And the ocean's five hours away.

So don't ever think you're a loser,
At worst you've just hit some bad form
You came to this world as a winner,
The moment your body was born.

OPPORTUNiTY iS AROUND THE CORNER

Opportunity comes, like buses that run,
Past the bus stop inside of your brain.
If you miss one, well that is a shame,
But don't worry another will come.

Stay alert and alive 'til the next one arrives,
And when it pulls in to your stop,
Hop on and head straight for the top.
Take your seat and hold on for the ride.

FiND YOUR CAVE OF BRAVE

You're braver than you think you are,
I know you don't believe it.
But there's a cave of brave inside,
Reserved for when you need it.

So find your reason to be brave,
And watch as bravery grows.
Take a look around your cave.
And see how deep it goes.

Be brave when fear finds you,
In the darkness of your house.
Be brave before your audience,
When words won't fit your mouth.

Be brave when someone's hurting,
And they need you to be strong.
Be brave when someone's doing something,
You perceive as wrong.

Be brave in your expression,
When you represent yourself.
Be brave in your opinions,
When you talk to someone else.

Be brave when opportunity,
Provides the perfect chance.
Be brave when love inspires you,
With a single passing glance.

Be brave when fortune finds you,
Make the choice to take its lead.
Sometimes a bit of bravery,
Is really all you need.

WORK YOUR SOCKS OFF

If you want to be a champion,
Or the captain of your team.
It's apparent natural talent's,
Advantageous to that dream.

But if you're born without it,
Then there is another way.
Ask anyone who's anyone,
And everyone will say.

A natural talent's wonderful,
The perfect place to start.
But if you want to be the best,
It's just a tiny part.

You have to work your socks off,
The blood, the sweat, the tears.
You have to work your socks off,
Even if it takes you years.

You have to work your socks off,
And here's the reason why.
Hard work can beat a talent,
If that talent doesn't try.

So go and work your socks off,
And blossom like a flower.
Talent's great, but working hard's,
Your secret superpower.

LiTTLE MiRACLES

If you're wanting to witness a miracle,
Don't mope around hoping one shows.
There are plenty already in motion,
Just look past the end of your nose.

Behold the mundane and atypical,
The wind as it whistles and blows.
The endless devotion of waves in the ocean,
The flower that aimlessly grows.

The forest of oak never planted,
The lure of the moon as it glows.
The beautiful hues of a sunrise,
From a pallet that nobody chose.

The miracles taken for granted,
The tap that continually flows.
The constant supplies of skinny french fries,
The scent of the single red rose.

The wheel that allows us to travel,
The brake we apply as it slows.
The fire that warms to your middle,
The weight of each flake as it snows.

The fortified walls of a castle,
A warning to all who oppose.
The brain that can fathom a riddle,
The foot that can wiggle its toes.

The galaxy's out in the distance,
So far away nobody goes.
And here we are part of the process,
For reasons that nobody knows.

So miracles are in existence,
They're just wearing ordinary clothes.
Perhaps now I've told you you'll notice,
Just look past the end of your nose.

START WiTH YOU

You can colour your hair,
Make it orange or blue.
You can buy brand new clothes,
Every weekend or two.
You can read up on culture,
And alter your view.
But whatever you do,
You will always be you.

So where do you start?
Well before the above.
Try making that person,
A person you love.
Don't focus on pretty,
Or handsome or wealthy.
No, focus on happy,
And helpful and healthy.

And learn to enjoy,
Spending time around you.
'Cause wherever you go,
You'll be going there too.
And be good to yourself,
Start today, not tomorrow.
Once you love who you are,
You'll find others will follow.

BE AMBiTiOUS

Ambition's a condition that will pay for your admission,
To a future you are hoping to achieve.
It's the spark to your ignition, it's the drive behind your vision,
It's the voice you hear that tells you to believe.

But beware! Too much ambition can result in bad decisions,
Taking chances that you wouldn't take before.
And success is not a given in a future yet unwritten,
So consider what to be ambitious for.

Be ambitious for time,
Be ambitious for peace.
Be ambitious for building,
Your own self-belief.

Be ambitious for laughter,
With friends you adore.
Be ambitious to live,
To one hundred and four.

Be ambitious for love,
Be ambitious for leisure.
For gusto, for joy,
And for moments of pleasure.

Build an empire of glee,
Build a kingdom of bliss.
Build a life for yourself,
That you won't want to miss.

Think big for today,
Even bigger tomorrow.
Ambition will lead you,
You just need to follow.

RESPECT YOURSELF

Before you're old, and set your mould, there's something you must do.

You must perfect, how to respect, the wonder that is you.

Care for yourself, before all else, and you should sail through.

For when you fail, to raise your sail, your boat will barely move.

Someone other, may take your rudder, insisting you approve.

New ropes attached, around your mast, they'll take you where they choose.

First it's great, to cross the lake, on someone else's steam.

Be careful though, you need to know, it's not all that it seems.

Sure you're cruising, but you're moving towards another's dreams.

You need respect, for your own deck, so grab your mop and pail.

Cherish your boat, untie your ropes, and learn to set your sail.

You are your captain, so make things happen, until the winds prevail.

The one thing I promise in life,

Is it's best to be honest in life.

No matter the season,

The person or reason,

A lie always comes at a price.

Sometimes the lie feels easy,

It's just a few words but believe me.

Those ill-planted seeds,

Quickly turn into weeds,

And they grow 'til they make you feel queasy.

And if you're not careful,
You'll spend your whole day,
Pruning and grooming,
To keep them at bay.

But they'll grip to your lips,
With each word that you say.
And they'll twist round your wrists,
And they'll lead you astray.

And the once simple truth,
Will slip further away.

So if there's a lie,
With its roots around you.
Don't cover its shoots,
With the sole of your shoe.

Just take a step backwards,
Be honest and true.
And pull it up quickly,
Before it grows through.

Then you can go home,
With no weeding to do.

DO YOUR BEST

There are moments in life when despite making plans,
The fate of your future is not in your hands.

And try as you might it cannot be controlled,
So you sit and you wait for your fate to unfold.

You might feel excitement, and worry, and doubt,
As they mix in your chest and they try to burst out.

But learn to be patient and stick to your plan,
Control every aspect you possibly can.

Show up with a smile, be on time, do your best,
And don't spend your days overthinking the rest.

For once you can say 'I've done all I can do',
If it doesn't work out, then it isn't on you.

HAVE HOPE

When you think you're at your bottom,
When an end comes to your rope.
When you're out amongst the ocean,
And there's water in your boat.
When you're close to giving up on things,
And feel like you can't cope.
Try to find one positive,
One thing that gives you hope.

And make that hope your beacon,
Let it guide you back to shore.
Make that hope your reason,
As you get up from the floor.
Let that hope surround you,
Like a light that frames a door.
And let that hope remind you,
Things are still worth fighting for.

BE THE **YOU** THAT YOU ARE

Your life has begun, so **BE**lieve in **YOU**rself,
You don't have to live it like **EVERYONE ELSE**.
The world **IS** your stage, you're **ALREADY** the star,
So be **HERE** without fear as the you that you are.

THE STAiRCASE
OF LiFE

The staircase of life is complex,
There's an endless collection of steps.
But if looking up,
Feels a little too much,
Concentrate on the one that comes next.

And after each step has been climbed,
Climb another and leave it behind.
Before very long,
You'll be where you belong,
If you take it one step at a time.

GET BACK UP

If you think you're failing,
At something you love,
And disaster is moments ahead.

Don't think of failing,
It does you no good,
Think about falling instead.

If you went out walking,
And you were to fall,
You might feel a little shook up.

You'd check you're still working,
And then all in all,
The next thing you'll do is get up.

You might feel embarrassed,
Perhaps you'll just laugh,
You may even shed the odd tear.

But after a moment,
The whole thing will pass,
And your journey resumes without fear.

But what you won't do,
Is stay on the floor,
Aghast as you loudly exclaim.

'I'm done with this walking, I tried!
But no more,
I'll never try walking again.'

So next time you fail,
Don't sit on your tail,
Get back to your feet and stand tall.

Success doesn't come,
To the ones who don't fail,
But the ones who get up when they fall.

SHARE YOUR FEELINGS

If you're angry or sad,
If life's driving you mad,
Find a way to express how you're feeling.

If you bottle things up,
There's a chance you'll get shook,
And EXPLODE! All over the ceiling.

GOODBYE
JEALOUSY

Jealousy's a monster, eyes of green and full of frowns,
It sits upon your shoulder and it tries to steal your crown.
It always tells you what you're not,
And all the things you haven't got,
It thinks about itself a lot, don't let it bring you down.

If monster whispers in your ear that someone's cut the line,
Or gets attention you do not, tell monster that you're fine.
Needs don't always come as par,
To get where you already are,
Another person may require more help and extra time.

If monster shows you someone else,
with whom you are impressed,
Instead of feeling jealous be inspired by their success.
Show monster a new point of view,
If they can do it so can you,
The dreams you have will not come true
by wishing they had less.

10 STEPS to a HAPPY LIFE

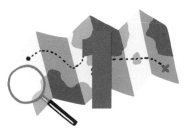

Step number one is make it fun,
Life's too short for boring.
Use your guile to make you smile,
Play games and go exploring.
Find a way to make each day,
A day that's worth adoring.

Step number two, live life as you,
Whoever 'you' may be.
Don't be a version of a person,
Others want to see.
Express yourself, impress yourself,
Be proud to say 'I'm me'.

Step number three, grow your own tree,
The world won't do it for you.
You have the seeds to grow your dreams,
So plant them! I implore you.
With love and luck, you'll raise them up,
Until they stand before you.

Step number four, you don't *need* more,
Learn to be happy with less.
Once you've freed that need for greed,
You'll let go of excess,
And quickly find you redefine,
Your rules of happiness.

Step number five, hard work and drive,
Builds lives you won't regret.
It may still take a lucky break,
To make it, but I'll bet,
The harder that you work at things,
The luckier you'll get.

Step number six, don't try to fix,
Your problems by yourself.
Learn to share with those who care,
About your mental health.
We walk our roads with lighter loads,
When walked with someone else.

Step number seven, learn a lesson,
From losses and mistakes.
Don't stamp your feet, meet each defeat,
With questions and debate.
And when you've found what let you down,
Go back and set it straight.

Step number eight is educate,
Your mind to be your own.
Make it required to be inspired,
By knowledge yet unknown.
Expand your brain until it reigns,
With wisdom as its throne.

Step number nine, of course, be kind,
For kindness is divine.
A pretty face that deals in hate,
Grows ugly over time.
But make compassion fashion,
And you'll always look sublime.

Step number ten is be the friend,
That you would want to know.
Be fun, be nice, exchange advice,
And when they need you, show.
Expect the same without refrain,
And watch your friendships grow.

And just in case ten's not enough, here comes another few,
Try to find the positives in everything you do.
Take a realistic, optimistic, futuristic view,
Be eccentric, be authentic, take a stand and see it through.

Live a life *you're* proud of,
That's the key to BEING YOU!

Published by Collins
An imprint of HarperCollins Publishers
Westerhill Road
Bishopbriggs
Glasgow G64 2QT

www.collins.co.uk

HarperCollins Publishers
Macken House
39/40 Mayor Street Upper
Dublin 1
Ireland D01 C9W8

First published 2023

Publisher: Michelle I'Anson • Editor: Beth Ralston • Designer: Kevin Robbins

A catalogue record for this book is
available from the British Library.

ISBN 978-0-00-858133-6

Printed in Latvia

10 9 8 7 6 5 4 3

This book contains FSC™ certified paper and other controlled
sources to ensure responsible forest management.

For more information visit: www.harpercollins.co.uk/green